This book is dedicated to **The Almighty God**, who has translated me from the kingdom of darkness into **the Kingdom of Light**.

From living as a believer yet participating in darkness, **HE** called me to live as a **Kingdom citizen on a mission**, walking with purpose and shining **HIS** marvellous light.

He is still writing my story…

To **the Author and Finisher of my Faith**, I give all glory and honour.

CONTENTS

What is the Kingdom of God...5

Jesus' Teachings about the Kingdom of God........................13

Aspects of the Kingdom of God

Ruler of the Kingdom of God: King Jesus................................115

Kingdom Citizenship...123

Kingdom Language & Communication..................................133

Kingdom Values & Beliefs..143

Kingdom Mindset..153

Kingdom Roles..163

Religion & Spirituality in the Kingdom....................................173

Kingdom Social Institutions...183

Kingdom Arts & Business..193

Kingdom Food & Health..203

Kingdom Finance..213

History of the Kingdom..223

Eternal Life in the Kingdom...233

Holy Spirit - The Kingdom Helper...243

True Kingdom Disciple..251

Fruit of the Spirit...261

Conclusion..271

Autobiography..272

What is the Kingdom of God

Introduction

Let us uncover the mysteries of the Kingdom of God.

I will begin with the foundation

Understanding the Kingdom of God.

Unless we understand this, our walk with God remains shallow. Jesus Himself preached one central message: *"Repent, for the Kingdom of God is at hand."* (Mark 1:15). Therefore, if this was His primary message, it must also be our foundation.

What is the Kingdom of God?

The Kingdom of God is not just a concept, but a reality.

In simple terms, the Kingdom of God is the rule and reign of God over His people, creation, and all of life.

It is God's government, God's authority, and God's way of doing things.

It is not limited to a physical location but is first a spiritual reality that manifests in the natural.

Jesus said in Luke 17:20-2 *"The Kingdom of God is not coming with signs to be observed; nor will they say, 'Look, here it is!' or 'There!' for behold, the kingdom of God is in your midst."*

This means the Kingdom begins within us when we submit to the rule of God in our hearts, but it also has a future dimension, the eternal reign of God in fullness.

Biblical Foundations of the Kingdom

Let's trace the Kingdom through Scripture:

Old Testament perspective

God is revealed as King throughout the Old Testament. Psalm 103:19 says: *"The Lord has established His throne in the heavens, and His kingdom rules over everything."*

Israel was called to be a kingdom of priests (Exodus 19:6). The whole story of Israel points to God's desire to rule through a chosen people.

The prophets foresaw a coming King, the **Messiah** who would establish an everlasting Kingdom (Isaiah 9:6-7; Daniel 7:13-14).

Economy:

Earthly kingdoms depend on resources that can run out.

God's Kingdom operates by faith and divine provision, where resources never run dry.

Application

Understanding the Kingdom is not about theory; it demands a response.

We must choose daily to submit to the King in every area of our lives.

We must be ambassadors, representing the Kingdom wherever we go

(2 Corinthians 5:20).

We must live with eternity in mind, knowing that this world is temporary, but the Kingdom of God is forever.

Source of authority:

Earthly kingdoms derive authority from men, constitutions, and armies.

The Kingdom of God derives authority from God Himself, who is eternal and sovereign.

Nature of rule:

Earthly kingdoms often operate through domination, oppression, and self-interest.

God's Kingdom operates through love, righteousness, peace, and joy in the Holy Spirit (Romans 14:17).

Citizenship:

In earthly kingdoms, citizenship is by birth or naturalization.

In God's Kingdom, citizenship comes by being *born again* (John 3:3).

Duration:

Earthly kingdoms rise and fall, but the Kingdom of God is everlasting (Daniel 2:44).

New Testament perspective

With the coming of Jesus, the Kingdom is announced and demonstrated. Jesus is the King, and through Him the Kingdom is made available.

He preached, healed the sick, cast out demons, and forgave sins, showing that the Kingdom had broken into human history.

In the Gospels, the Kingdom is both present ("the Kingdom is at hand") and future ("Your Kingdom come").

The apostles continued this message, proclaiming the good news of the Kingdom and preparing believers for its fullness when Christ returns (Acts 28:30-31).

The Difference Between the Kingdom of God and Earthly Kingdoms

It is important to understand that God's Kingdom is unlike any kingdom of this world.

Jesus' Teachings about the Kingdom of God

Luke 4:43 "I must proclaim the good news of the Kingdom of God, because that is why I was sent."

When Jesus spoke these words, He was revealing the heartbeat of His mission. He did not come to establish a religion, a club, or a temporary movement. He came to bring the **Kingdom of God** into the earth, a Kingdom that transforms hearts, renews minds, and restores God's original intent for humanity.

The Kingdom is the Priority

Jesus said, "I must…" Not "I should", not "I might", but "I must."

This is the urgency of the Kingdom. The Gospel is not an optional side project; it is the very reason Heaven invaded earth through Christ. We cannot call ourselves followers of the King if His priority is not our priority.

The Kingdom is Good News

The good news is not just that we get to go to Heaven someday, it's that Heaven's culture can invade our lives now. Where there was

sickness, the Kingdom brings healing. Where there was oppression, the Kingdom brings freedom. Where there was lack, the Kingdom brings abundance. This Gospel is the announcement that the King has come, and His rule changes everything.

The Kingdom is a Commission

If Jesus was sent to proclaim the Kingdom, and we are sent as His body in the world, then our mission is the same. We are ambassadors, carriers of Heaven's authority, witnesses to the King's love and power. We are not here to blend in, we are here to bring the Kingdom into boardrooms, classrooms, marketplaces, and neighbourhoods.

If the Son of God said, "I must proclaim the good news of the Kingdom of God," how much more should we? Let's make a decision to align our voices, our time, and our resources with the King's mandate. The world is desperate for the reality of God's Kingdom. And we, you and I, are the ones entrusted to proclaim it......

If this was the heartbeat of Jesus, it must be your heartbeat as a Kingdom Citizen. Wherever you go, your workplace, your home, your neighbourhood you are carrying the Kingdom. Speak it. Live it. Show it. The world doesn't just need our opinions; it needs the King and His Kingdom.

The Kingdom of God is Like a Sower

- Matthew 13:3, Mark 4:3, Luke 8:5 –

Jesus often spoke in parables because the Kingdom of God is too rich to be captured in one definition. I will now explore, "The Kingdom of God is like a Sower who went out to sow."

Notice the Kingdom is not described as a palace, a throne, or even a crown. It is described as a Sower. Why? Because the Kingdom comes through seed, and seed is meant to multiply.

The Kingdom Comes as Seed

Seeds look small, but inside them is destiny. The Word of God, when planted in a heart, carries the power to transform lives, families, and nations. Don't despise the small beginnings. Every great move of God started with a seed.

The Kingdom Depends on Soil

The same seed fell on four kinds of soil: the path, the rocky ground, the thorns, and the good soil. The problem was never the seed the problem was always the soil. In other words, the issue is not with the Kingdom, it's with the condition of the heart receiving it. What kind of soil are you?

The Kingdom Produces Fruit

When the seed falls on good soil, it produces thirty, sixty, even a hundredfold. That is the nature of the Kingdom, it multiplies. The Kingdom is not just about hearing the Word; it's about bearing fruit that transforms lives. A Kingdom person is a fruitful person.

___

When Jesus says, "The Kingdom of God is like a Sower," He is telling us: The Kingdom is not passive it's active, it's sowing, it's multiplying. The seed of the Word is available for all, but the question is: will your heart be good soil?

___

The Kingdom of God is Like (the *Parable of the Weeds*)

Matthew 13:24-25 "The Kingdom of Heaven is like a man who sowed good seed in his field. But while everyone was sleeping, his enemy came and sowed weeds among the wheat and went away."

Jesus never wasted words when describing the Kingdom. He says, "The Kingdom of God is like a man who sowed good seed in his field." But while everyone was sleeping, the enemy came and planted weeds among the wheat.

This story is not just about farming it is about life in the Kingdom. It shows us three truths we must never forget.

The Kingdom is Always Sowing Good Seed

God's Kingdom is good seed truth, life, peace, righteousness. Wherever His Word is planted, it brings hope and transformation. But notice this: while the seed was good, the enemy was also busy planting counterfeit seed. The Kingdom of God is advancing, but it always faces opposition.

The Kingdom and the Counterfeit Grow Together

The servants asked, "Should we pull out the weeds?" But the master said, "No, let them grow together until the harvest." That tells us that in this world, the true and the false, the genuine and the fake, will grow side by side. Don't be discouraged when you see weeds around you, it doesn't mean the Kingdom is failing. It means the harvest is coming.

The Kingdom is Proven at Harvest Time

At the end, the master said, "First collect the weeds and tie them in bundles to be burned; then gather the wheat and bring it into my barn." The Kingdom of God is about endurance and fruitfulness. You don't need to fight every weed in your life. Just stay rooted, keep growing, and at harvest time, the fruit will speak for you.

When Jesus says, "The Kingdom of God is like the parable of the weeds," He's teaching us patience, perspective, and confidence. The wheat will always outlast the weeds, and the King Himself will separate the true from the false. Our job is not to panic but to keep bearing fruit until the harvest

The Kingdom of God is Like a Mustard Seed

Matthew 13:31–32 "The Kingdom of Heaven is like a mustard seed, which a man took and planted in his field. Though it is the smallest of all seeds, yet when it grows, it is the largest of garden plants and becomes a tree, so that the birds come and perch in its branches."

Jesus chose one of the tiniest seeds to reveal the greatness of the Kingdom. Why? Because the **Kingdom of God** doesn't always come with noise and drama, it often begins small, hidden, and overlooked. But what starts as insignificant grows into something unstoppable.

The Kingdom Starts Small but Carries Power

A mustard seed is tiny, but inside it lies potential for greatness. The **Kingdom of God** in your life may look small one prayer, one word, one act of faith. Don't despise it. The seed may be small, but the God behind it is big.

The Kingdom Grows Beyond Expectation

Jesus says the seed becomes the largest of garden plants, even a tree. That means the Kingdom doesn't remain where it starts. It expands, it influences, it takes over. The more you allow the Word of God to grow in you, the more your life becomes a testimony of Kingdom increase.

The Kingdom Brings Shelter and Blessing

When the mustard tree grows, birds come to perch in its branches. That's a picture of influence, your life rooted in the Kingdom, becomes a refuge for others. People will find rest, hope, and covering because you allowed the seed of the Kingdom to grow.

When Jesus says, "The Kingdom of God is like a mustard seed," He's reminding us: never underestimate small beginnings. If you carry the seed of the Kingdom, you already carry greatness. Stay faithful, stay planted, and watch God turn your seed into a tree that blesses nations.

The Kingdom of God is Like Yeast

Matthew 13:33 "The Kingdom of Heaven is like yeast that a woman took and mixed into about sixty pounds of flour until it worked all through the dough."

Jesus uses something as ordinary as yeast to describe the extraordinary nature of the Kingdom. Yeast is small and hidden, but once it is mixed into the dough, it cannot be stopped. In the same way, the **Kingdom of God** may look small or invisible at first but once it is planted, it transforms everything it touches.

The Kingdom Works Quietly but Powerfully

Yeast doesn't make noise, but it makes impact. The Kingdom is not always loud and dramatic, sometimes it is subtle, working in the background of your life, changing attitudes, renewing minds, and shaping character. Don't mistake silence for inactivity, God's Kingdom is at work in you even when you can't see it.

The Kingdom Influences Everything It Touches

Jesus said the yeast worked "all through the dough." That means the Kingdom doesn't stay in one corner of your life. It spreads into your relationships, your finances, your decisions, your community. When the Kingdom enters, it doesn't just visit, it takes over.

The Kingdom Brings Transformation

Just as dough cannot remain the same once yeast is added, life cannot remain the same once the Kingdom takes root. The Kingdom turns brokenness into wholeness, despair into hope, and weakness into strength. Transformation is the evidence that the yeast of the Kingdom is alive in you.

When Jesus says, "The Kingdom of God is like yeast," He is teaching us this: the Kingdom may start small and hidden, but it is unstoppable, irresistible, and transformational. The question is - have you allowed the yeast of the Kingdom to work through your whole life?

The Kingdom of God is Like Hidden Treasure

Matthew 13:44 "The Kingdom of Heaven is like treasure hidden in a field. When a man found it, he hid it again, and then in his joy went and sold all he had and bought that field."

Jesus compares the Kingdom of God to hidden treasure. Why treasure? Because the Kingdom is not cheap, it is not common, and it is not found on the surface. It is priceless, precious, and worth everything.

The Kingdom is Discovered, Not Invented

The man didn't create the treasure he discovered it. The **Kingdom of God** is not man's idea; it is God's reality. You don't build it with your own wisdom; you uncover it through revelation. That's why we pray, "Lord, open our eyes!"

The Kingdom Demands Total Surrender

When the man found the treasure, he sold everything with joy. Notice this, he didn't mourn his sacrifice; he rejoiced because what he was gaining was far greater than what he was losing. The Kingdom requires giving up lesser things to gain the greatest thing: Christ and His rule.

The Kingdom Brings True Joy

This man wasn't forced to buy the field; he did it with joy. That's the Kingdom, it's not drudgery, it's delight. When you truly encounter the King, serving Him is not a burden, it's a privilege. The joy of the Kingdom is greater than the pleasures of the world.

When Jesus says, "The **Kingdom of God** is like hidden treasure," He is reminding us: the Kingdom is worth everything. Don't settle for surface living. Dig deep, pursue Christ, and be willing to surrender all, because in Him you gain more than the world could ever offer.

The Kingdom of God is Like a Net

Matthew 13:47–48 "Once again, the Kingdom of Heaven is like a net that was let down into the lake and caught all kinds of fish. When it was full, the fishermen pulled it up on the shore. Then they sat down and collected the good fish in baskets but threw the bad away."

Jesus gives us another picture of the Kingdom: a net. Unlike a hook that catches one fish at a time, a net gathers many. This is a prophetic image of the Kingdom's reach, wide, inclusive, and unstoppable.

The Kingdom Reaches All Kinds

The net caught "all kinds of fish." That means the Kingdom is not for one tribe, one race, one class, or one background. The Kingdom is for the poor and the rich, the weak and the strong, the broken and the whole. Nobody is beyond the reach of the King's net.

The Kingdom is Patient Until Fullness

The net wasn't pulled up until it was full. That speaks of God's patience. He is giving the world time to respond, time for more souls to enter. Don't mistake God's patience for absence He is waiting, not sleeping. The harvest is certain.

The Kingdom Brings Separation

At the shore, the good fish were kept, and the bad were thrown away. That is the reality of the Kingdom: it is inclusive in invitation but exclusive in outcome. Everyone is caught in the net, but only those who have truly submitted to the King will remain. The final separation is not in man's hands it is in God's.

When Jesus says, "The **Kingdom of God** is like a net," He is reminding us that His Kingdom is wide in reach, patient in timing, but final in judgment. The net is already in the water. The question is not whether you are caught, the question is whether you will be found faithful when the net is pulled in.

The Kingdom of God is Like a Pearl

Matthew 13:45–46 "Again, the Kingdom of Heaven is like a merchant looking for fine pearls. When he found one of great value, he went away and sold everything he had and bought it."

Jesus gives us another picture of the Kingdom **a pearl of great price**. The pearl is precious, costly, and beautiful. It represents the incomparable worth of the Kingdom of God, something worth trading everything else for.

The Kingdom Requires a Seeker's Heart

The merchant was searching for pearls. He wasn't passive; he was intentional. The Kingdom is discovered by those who seek. Scripture says, "Seek first the Kingdom of God…" If you're casual with the Kingdom, you won't uncover its true value.

The Kingdom Surpasses Every Other Value

The merchant had seen many pearls, but when he found this one, he recognized it was different. The Kingdom is not just another option on the shelf of life; it is the one thing that surpasses all. Nothing else can compare to the reign of God in your life.

The Kingdom Demands Total Surrender

The merchant sold everything to gain the pearl. Notice this, he didn't lose, he gained. The Kingdom is worth your whole life, your time, your resources, your dreams. Anything you lay down for the Kingdom is never wasted; it is an exchange for something far greater.

When Jesus says, "The **Kingdom of God** is like a pearl," He is teaching us that the Kingdom is not cheap, not common, not ordinary — it is priceless. The question today is: have you recognized its value, and are you willing to give everything for it?

The Kingdom of God is Like Workers in a Vineyard

Scripture: Matthew 20:1–16 "For the Kingdom of Heaven is like a landowner who went out early in the morning to hire workers for his vineyard…"

Jesus paints a picture of the Kingdom that challenges our human sense of fairness. He says the Kingdom of God is like a landowner who hired workers at different hours of the day, some early in the morning, others at noon, and even some at the last hour yet they all received the same reward.

This parable isn't about wages. It's about grace. It's about the heart of the King.

The Kingdom Calls at Different Times

The landowner went out morning, midday, and evening. That's the heart of God! The Kingdom is always reaching, always inviting. Some come to Christ early in life; others come at the last moment, but all are welcome. The Kingdom doesn't reject latecomers; it redeems them.

The Kingdom Operates by Grace, Not Comparison

When those who worked all day saw others getting the same pay, they grumbled. But the master said, "Friend, I am not being unfair to you... Are you envious because I am generous?"

That's the Kingdom; it's not built on human fairness but divine generosity. Stop comparing your journey to others. The reward is not about how long you've worked; it's about who you're working for.

The Kingdom Rewards Faithfulness, Not Position

The last became first, and the first became last. That means in the Kingdom, it's not about status or seniority; it's about obedience. The ones who answered the call, no matter the hour, received the same grace. God is not impressed by how early you started; He's looking for how faithfully you finish.

When Jesus says, "The Kingdom of God is like workers in a vineyard," He's showing us that the Kingdom is not earned, it's received. It's not about performance, it's about purpose. It's not about who started first, it's about who stays faithful to the end.

The Kingdom of God is Like a Wedding Banquet

Matthew 22:1-2 *"The Kingdom of Heaven is like a king who prepared a wedding banquet for his son."*

When Jesus compares the Kingdom to a wedding banquet, He is showing us the heart of God; a King who prepares a feast, not a famine. The Kingdom is not dull or distant; it is a celebration! The King has made everything ready, and His greatest desire is that we come and dine with Him.

But in this story, we see something shocking, many who were invited refused to come. They were too busy, too distracted, too comfortable. Yet the King's plan continued, because in the Kingdom, rejection doesn't stop purpose!

The Kingdom is an Invitation, Not an Obligation

The King *invited* guests; He didn't force them. The Kingdom operates through invitation. God won't drag anyone to the table, but His arms are always open. Every time you hear the Word, Heaven is sending you an invitation: *"Come, everything is ready!"*

The Kingdom Includes the Unexpected

When the first invitees rejected the call, the King sent His servants to the streets to gather *"everyone they could find; both good and bad."*

That's grace! The Kingdom is not for the perfect; it's for the willing. God is filling His banquet with people the world overlooked, because what qualifies you is not your record, but your response.

The Kingdom Requires the Right Garment

When the King entered, He found one guest without wedding clothes. That garment represents righteousness, being clothed in Christ. You can't just show up; you must be transformed. The Kingdom is not just about attendance; it's about alignment. You can't wear the world's clothes at the King's table.

When Jesus says, *"The Kingdom of God is like a wedding banquet,"* He's reminding us: the invitation has been sent, the table is ready, and the feast is waiting. Don't be too busy, too proud, or too distracted to answer the call. The King has prepared something greater than you can imagine, but you must come dressed in His righteousness.

The Kingdom of God Is Like Ten Virgins

Matthew 25:1 *"Then the Kingdom of Heaven will be like ten virgins who took their lamps and went out to meet the bridegroom."*

When Jesus speaks of the Kingdom being like ten virgins, He's showing us a picture of readiness. All ten were invited, all ten had lamps, all ten were waiting for the bridegroom, but only five were wise. Why? Because only five carried oil in their lamps.

This parable isn't about who started waiting; it's about who stayed ready.

The Kingdom Is for the Prepared, Not the Present

All ten virgins were present, but only five were prepared. Being around the things of God doesn't mean you are ready for the move of God. The Kingdom separates those who are casual from those who are committed. The oil represents intimacy, prayer, and the presence of the Holy Spirit, things that cannot be borrowed or shared.

The Delay Reveals the Depth

The bridegroom took longer than expected,

and all became drowsy. But the difference was this: when the call came at midnight *"Here's the bridegroom!"* only those who had oil could rise and shine. The delay didn't destroy them; it exposed them. In the Kingdom, delay is never denial, it's a test of preparation.

The Door Closes for the Unready

When the foolish virgins tried to borrow oil, the wise said, *"No, there may not be enough for both us and you."* By the time they went to buy, the door was shut. The Kingdom has an open invitation, but not an open door forever. Grace is available now, but preparation is our responsibility.

When Jesus says, *"The Kingdom of God is like ten virgins,"* He is telling us: stay ready. Keep your oil full. Keep your flame burning. Don't wait until the midnight cry to start preparing, live ready every day. Because when the King comes, it will be too late to go shopping for oil.

The Kingdom of God Is Like a Man Going on a Journey

Matthew 25:14 *"Again, the Kingdom of Heaven is like a man going on a journey, who called his servants and entrusted his wealth to them."*

When Jesus says the Kingdom of God is like a man going on a journey, He's describing a Kingdom of trust, responsibility, and reward. The master represents God. The servants represent us. The talents represent everything He has placed in our hands, time, gifts, influence, and opportunities.

The question of the Kingdom is not *"What did you receive?"* but *"What did you do with what you received?"*

The Kingdom Entrusts Us with Purpose

The master gave talents *"to each according to his ability."* That means in the Kingdom, no one is empty-handed. Every believer carries a divine deposit. You may not have what others have, but you have what Heaven assigned to you, and it's enough to multiply.

The Kingdom Expects Fruitfulness, Not Excuses

Two servants took what they had and doubled

it. The third buried his talent and blamed fear. The master's response was strong: *"You wicked and lazy servant."*

Why? Because in the Kingdom, fear is not an excuse for fruitlessness. God is not looking for perfection; He's looking for productivity. The Kingdom grows when you use what you've been given.

The Kingdom Rewards Faithfulness, Not Volume

Notice; the master gave the same praise to both servants who multiplied their talents: *"Well done, good and faithful servant."* One had five, one had two, but both were faithful. The Kingdom doesn't measure by size; it measures by stewardship. Faithfulness is Heaven's currency.

When Jesus says, "*The Kingdom of God is like a man who went on a journey,*" He's reminding us: everything you have is a trust from Heaven. Don't bury it. Don't hide it. Don't waste it. Use it, multiply it, and when the Master returns, He will say, "*Well done, good and faithful servant, enter into the joy of your Lord.*"

The Kingdom of God Is Like the Final Judgment

Matthew 25:31–32 *"When the Son of Man comes in His glory, and all the angels with Him, He will sit on His glorious throne. All the nations will be gathered before Him, and He will separate the people one from another as a shepherd separates the sheep from the goats."*

When Jesus describes the Kingdom as a scene of judgment, He's showing us that the Kingdom is not just about power, it's about accountability. It's not just about grace received; it's also about fruit produced. The Kingdom begins with invitation but ends with evaluation.

This is not a parable to frighten us., it's a revelation to wake us up.

The Kingdom Reveals the King in His Glory

Jesus says, *"When the Son of Man comes in His glory."* The same Jesus who walked in humility will return in majesty. The Kingdom may look hidden now, but one day it will be visible to all. Every crown will fall, every throne will bow, and every heart will see the King in His glory.

The Kingdom Separates by Evidence, Not by Titles

The King separates sheep from goats, not based on church attendance, but by Kingdom action. He says, "I was hungry, and you fed Me. I was a stranger, and you invited Me in." In other words, Kingdom faith produces Kingdom fruit. The evidence of your faith is how you treat people. The way you serve the least is the way you honor the King.

The Kingdom Rewards Compassion, Not Complacency

The sheep didn't even realize they were serving the King; their compassion was genuine, not performative. The goats, on the other hand, ignored opportunities to show love. The Kingdom is not about how loudly you worship, but how deeply you love. Every act of mercy is ministry to the King Himself.

So when Jesus says, *"The Kingdom of God is like the final judgment,"* He's telling us: live ready, live right, and live with love. One day, the King will separate words from works, religion from relationship, and form from fruit. Let your life prove that you belong to the Kingdom, not just by what you believe, but by how you live.

The Kingdom of God Is a Mystery

Mark 4:11 – *"To you it has been given to know the mystery of the Kingdom of God; but to those outside, everything is said in parables."*

When Jesus spoke of the mystery of the Kingdom, He was revealing something powerful, the Kingdom of God is not discovered by human wisdom, but by divine revelation. The Kingdom is not hidden *from* us; it is hidden *for* us, for those with eyes to see and ears to hear.

The Kingdom is a mystery, not because God wants to confuse you, but because He wants to reveal Himself to those who are hungry.

The Kingdom Is Hidden from the Casual but Revealed to the Committed

Jesus said, *"To you it has been given..."* meaning the revelation of the Kingdom is a gift to disciples, not to spectators. The crowd hears parables, but disciples hear purpose. The Kingdom requires intimacy, not just curiosity. If you stay close to the King, you will understand the Kingdom.

The Kingdom Works from the Inside Out

A mystery means something unseen is at work. Just as a seed grows underground before it breaks the surface, the Kingdom works within before it manifests without. Don't be discouraged when you don't see visible results yet, the Kingdom is growing silently inside you. Transformation begins in secret before it becomes public.

The Kingdom Demands Spiritual Perception

Many hear the Word but miss the meaning. The difference is not in the message; it's in the mindset. Only those who approach the Word with hunger and humility can catch the revelation. The Kingdom cannot be grasped intellectually; it must be received spiritually. Revelation is Heaven's language.

When Jesus says, *"The Kingdom of God is a mystery,"* He is reminding us that the Kingdom is not about religion, it's about revelation. It's not about seeing with the natural eye but perceiving with the Spirit. To walk in the Kingdom, you must go beyond information and step into illumination.

The Kingdom of God Is Like a Growing Seed

Mark 4:26–27 – *"This is what the Kingdom of God is like. A man scatters seed on the ground. Night and day, whether he sleeps or gets up, the seed sprouts and grows, though he does not know how."*

Jesus compares the Kingdom of God to something so simple, yet so powerful, a seed. He shows us that the Kingdom doesn't come by force or speed, but by growth. It starts small, it works silently, but it produces powerfully.

The Kingdom is not in a hurry, but it is unstoppable.

The Kingdom Has Its Own Life Within It

The man plants the seed, then goes to sleep, but the seed keeps growing, *"he does not know how."* That's the mystery of the Kingdom! The Word of God carries divine life. Once it's planted in your heart, it begins to grow beyond your understanding. Even when you can't see it, it's working.

You may not know *how* God will do it, but the Kingdom guarantees that He *will*.

The Kingdom Grows in Stages, Not Instantly

Jesus says, *"First the blade, then the head, then the full grain in the head."* That means

Kingdom growth is progressive, not instant. Don't be discouraged by small beginnings, the process is proof that the seed is alive. Keep watering your faith, keep declaring the Word, because growth is happening even when you don't see change.

The Kingdom Starts Small but Ends Great

Then Jesus adds, *"It is like a mustard seed… though it is the smallest of all seeds, yet when it grows, it becomes the largest of garden plants."*
The Kingdom always expands, it multiplies, it influences, it transforms. What starts as a whisper of faith becomes a mighty tree of impact. Never underestimate what God has planted in you.

When Jesus says, *"The Kingdom of God is like a growing seed,"* He is teaching us this: the Kingdom is alive, it's active, and it's advancing. You might not see it now, but Heaven's seed inside you is maturing. Just stay faithful, because the Kingdom always finishes what it starts.

The Kingdom of God Is Not of This World

John 18:36 – *"Jesus answered, 'My Kingdom is not of this world. If it were, my servants would fight to prevent my arrest by the Jewish leaders. But now my Kingdom is from another place.'"*

When Jesus stood before Pilate, He was not defending Himself, He was defining His Kingdom. He said, *"My Kingdom is not of this world."*
In other words, *"I operate from a higher realm."* The Kingdom of God is not built on politics, power, or human systems. It is a Kingdom that cannot be shaken, corrupted, or controlled.

The Kingdom of God is a higher government, a divine order that rules over every other rule.

The Kingdom Has a Different Source

Jesus said, *"My Kingdom is not of this world."* That means the Kingdom doesn't come from human effort, it comes from Heaven's authority. The systems of this world rise and fall, but the Kingdom of God remains forever. You are not a citizen of chaos; you are an ambassador of a divine order.

When you know where your Kingdom comes from, you stop panicking like the world, because your supply, your peace, your power come from another realm!

The Kingdom Operates by a Different Spirit

Worldly kingdoms are built by control, conflict, and competition. But the Kingdom of God is built by love, truth, and righteousness. Jesus said, *"If my Kingdom were of this world, my servants would fight."*
The Kingdom doesn't advance through swords and strength, it advances through submission and Spirit. We don't conquer by fear; we conquer by faith.

The Kingdom Produces a Different People

To belong to this Kingdom means you are not ordinary. You carry Heaven's DNA. You live by Kingdom principles, speak Kingdom language, and carry Kingdom authority.
When the world says "impossible," the Kingdom says "done." When the world says "defeated," the Kingdom says "victorious."

You are in the world, but you are not of it.

When Jesus says, *"My Kingdom is not of this world,"* He is calling us to live from a higher reality. Don't let the noise of the world drown the voice of the King. You belong to a Kingdom that cannot be shaken, led by a King who cannot be defeated, and fuelled by a Spirit that cannot be stopped.

The Kingdom of God Is Righteousness, Peace, and Joy

Romans 14:17 – *"For the Kingdom of God is not a matter of eating and drinking, but of righteousness, peace and joy in the Holy Spirit."*

Paul reminds us here that the Kingdom of God is not about external rituals, it's about internal reality. The Kingdom is not built on what's on your plate, but what's in your heart. It's not about religious activity; it's about spiritual reality.

The Kingdom of God is not physical, it's spiritual, it's supernatural, and it's alive inside of you through the Holy Spirit!

The Kingdom Is Righteousness, the Right Standing

The first mark of the Kingdom is righteousness. That means to be in right relationship with God, not by your own effort, but through Christ Jesus. When you walk in the Kingdom, you don't live condemned, you live cleansed. You don't perform for acceptance; you live from acceptance.

The Kingdom begins when you stop trying to earn what Christ already gave you: right standing before God.

The Kingdom Is Peace, the Right Atmosphere

Where the Kingdom is, peace reigns. Peace is not the absence of problems, it's the presence of divine order.
Even when the storm rages, the King is still in control. Kingdom peace means you can stand firm while others panic, because you know who rules your heart.
The peace of the Kingdom is not external calm, it's internal confidence.

The Kingdom Is Joy, the Right Expression

Joy is the sound of the Kingdom! It is the overflow of the Holy Spirit. This joy doesn't come from circumstances; it flows from communion with God.
The world's happiness depends on what happens, but Kingdom joy depends on who's inside you. Joy is a Kingdom weapon; it keeps you strong when life tries to break you.

When Paul says, *"The Kingdom of God is not eating and drinking,"* he's reminding us that the Kingdom is not about religion, it's about relationship.

It's not about what's outside you, it's about what's inside you. Righteousness gives you position; peace gives you stability, and joy gives you strength.

That's what it means to live as a citizen of the Kingdom of God, to carry Heaven's reality everywhere you go.

The Kingdom of God Is Power

---

1 Corinthians 4:20 – *"For the Kingdom of God is not a matter of talk but of power."*

When Paul spoke these words, he was reminding the Church that the Kingdom of God is not about empty speech, but about demonstrated power.
The Kingdom is not a philosophy to be discussed, it is a reality to be displayed. It is not words that change lives, but the power of the King working through His people.

We are not called to explain the Kingdom only; we are called to express it.

The Kingdom Is Power to Transform Lives

The Kingdom doesn't come in fancy words; it comes in power that transforms. When the Kingdom comes, sickness leaves, chains break, and darkness flees.
The same Spirit that raised Jesus from the dead lives in you, that's Kingdom power!
The Kingdom is not theory; it's testimony. When people encounter you, they should encounter the evidence of the Kingdom.

The Kingdom Is Power to Overcome Sin and Fear

Many can talk about holiness, but only the power of the Holy Spirit can produce it.
The Kingdom empowers you to live above what used to control you. You no longer live defeated; you live dominion minded.
Kingdom citizens don't speak like victims; they walk like victors. Because where the Kingdom reigns, sin loses its grip, and fear loses its voice.

The Kingdom Is Power to Represent Heaven on Earth

We are not ordinary people, we are ambassadors of a powerful Kingdom.
Everywhere you go, your home, your workplace, your city, becomes an embassy of Heaven.
When you speak, Heaven backs you. When you pray, power moves. When you act in faith, the supernatural responds.
The world doesn't need more talkers, it needs Kingdom carriers.

When Paul says, *"The Kingdom of God is not a matter of talk but of power,"* he's calling the Church to move beyond words into works, beyond religion into revelation, beyond form into fire.

The Kingdom of God is real, alive, and active, and that same power is living in you right now.

The Kingdom of God Requires New Birth

John 3:3–5 – *"Jesus answered him, 'Very truly I tell you, no one can see the Kingdom of God unless they are born again… born of water and the Spirit.'"*

Nicodemus came to Jesus as a religious leader, but he didn't understand the Kingdom. Jesus shocked him: *"Unless one is born again, he cannot enter the Kingdom of God."*
The Kingdom is not inherited, not earned, and not observed from the outside. Entry requires spiritual birth, a radical transformation that only God can do.

The Kingdom begins not in your circumstances, but in your spirit.

The Kingdom Requires a Radical Inner Change

Being born again means starting over from the inside. It's not a ritual; it's a reality.
Your heart, mind, and spirit are recreated. Old habits, old sins, and old patterns are replaced by a new life in Christ. The Kingdom doesn't just change your life outwardly; it changes your DNA spiritually.

The Kingdom Is Accessed Through Water and Spirit

Jesus says, *"Born of water and the Spirit."* Water represents cleansing and repentance, turning away from sin. Spirit represents empowerment and life, God's presence dwelling in you. You can't enter the Kingdom with religion alone, but you can with repentance and revival. True Kingdom life comes when God's Spirit moves inside a cleansed heart.

The Kingdom Brings New Vision and Life

When you are born again, you can see the Kingdom. Nicodemus was a learned man, but he couldn't perceive Kingdom reality until he was reborn. Kingdom citizens see life differently, they see God's agenda, God's opportunities, and God's power operating in the world.

When Jesus says, *"Unless one is born again, he cannot enter the Kingdom of God,"* He is calling us to personal transformation. The Kingdom is not about religion, morality, or ritual, it's about rebirth. It's about life from Heaven entering your heart today.

The Kingdom of God Is Near

Mark 1:15 – *"The time has come," he said. "The Kingdom of God has come near. Repent and believe the good news!"*

Jesus announced a message that shook the world: *"The Kingdom of God is near!"* Not tomorrow, not someday, but now. Heaven is not distant; it is at your door. God's reign is not a concept; it is a reality breaking into our world today.

The Kingdom is near, and that changes how we live, think, and move.

The Kingdom Brings Urgency

Jesus said, *"Repent and believe the good news!"* The Kingdom is near, so there is no time to delay. Life is short, the enemy is active, and every moment counts. Kingdom living requires immediate response, repentance, obedience, and alignment with God's will.

The Kingdom Brings Transformation

The nearness of the Kingdom means that Heaven's power is ready to work in your life. Sickness can be healed, chains can be broken, fear can be overcome, the Kingdom doesn't wait for the future, it operates now. Wherever the Kingdom touches, lives are transformed.

The Kingdom Calls for Participation

The Kingdom is near, but it is not automatic. Jesus calls us to step in, to participate in prayer, service, and faith. Heaven is at work, and we are invited to join the advance. The nearness of the Kingdom demands that we live Kingdom lives today, not later.

When Jesus says, *"The Kingdom of God is near,"* He is telling us: get ready, step up, and live in His reality. Don't wait for the world to change; let your life reflect the presence of the King now. The Kingdom is not coming, it is here, and it is near.

Aspects of the Kingdom of God

Ruler of the Kingdom of God – KING JESUS

Every kingdom has a ruler, and without the King, there is no kingdom. If we are to understand God's Kingdom, we must first know and submit to the King who reigns over it.

Jesus as the Eternal King

The Scriptures reveal that Jesus is not just a religious leader or prophet, He is the eternal King.

Isaiah 9:6-7 prophesies: *For to us a child is born, to us a son is given,
and the government will be on his shoulders. And he will be called Wonderful Counsellor, Mighty God, Everlasting Father, Prince of Peace.*

*Of the greatness of his government and peace
there will be no end. He will reign on David's throne and over his kingdom, establishing and upholding it with*

justice and righteousness from that time on and forever. The zeal of the Lord Almighty will accomplish this."

His Kingship is not temporary like earthly rulers; it is everlasting (Hebrews 1:8 – *"Your throne, O God, is forever and ever."*).

From eternity past to eternity future, Jesus is the sovereign King.

His Authority, Reign, and Relationship with His People

- His Authority

After His resurrection, Jesus declared: *"All authority in heaven and on earth has been given to me"* (Matthew 28:18).

His authority is supreme and unmatched, over nature, demons, sickness, sin, and even death.

Philippians 2:9-11 tells us that every knee will bow and every tongue confess that Jesus Christ is Lord.

His Reign

Jesus reigns not by oppression but by righteousness, love, and truth.

Romans 14:17: *"The kingdom of God is not eating and drinking, but righteousness, peace, and joy in the Holy Spirit."*

Unlike earthly kings who tax and burden their people, Jesus brings rest: *"Come to me, all you who are weary and burdened, and I will give you rest"* (Matthew 11:28).

His Relationship with His People

Jesus is not a distant King, He is personal. He calls us friends in (John 15:15), yet we also honor Him as Lord.

As our Shepherd King (John 10:11), He lays down His life for His sheep.

We are citizens of His Kingdom, but also children of God through adoption (Ephesians 2:19). This makes our relationship with Him both royal and intimate.

The Kingdom Inaugurated Through Christ's Life, Death, and Resurrection

The Kingdom of God became a present reality through Jesus' coming.

His Life: Through His teachings, miracles, and example, He demonstrated Kingdom living. The blind saw, the lame walked, and the oppressed were set free. These were signs that the Kingdom had arrived.

His Death: On the cross, He broke the power of sin and Satan. Colossians 2:15 says He disarmed principalities and powers, triumphing over them. The cross was not defeat; it was the coronation of our King.

His Resurrection: The resurrection was the ultimate victory. It marked the inauguration of the Kingdom in power. By rising, He proved He is King not only of the living but also of the dead.

Acts 2:36 proclaims: *"God has made this Jesus, whom you crucified, both Lord and Christ."*

Therefore, the Kingdom we belong to is not an idea, but a living reality made possible by Christ's victory.

Application

Recognize Jesus as King, He is not just Savior but Lord. This means submitting every area of our lives to His rule.

Live under His authority, Obedience is the mark of Kingdom citizens. His commands are not burdensome but life-giving.

Reflect Kingdom life, As His people, we are ambassadors who must carry His love, peace, and righteousness wherever we go.

Summary

Jesus as the Eternal King, His throne is everlasting; His rule is unshakable.

His Authority, Reign, and Relationship, He reigns in righteousness, not oppression; He has all authority in heaven and earth; and He relates to us not only as Lord but also as friend and Shepherd.

The Kingdom Inaugurated, Through His life, Jesus demonstrated the Kingdom; through His death, He defeated sin and Satan; and through His resurrection, He established the Kingdom in power.

Questions for you to Reflect on

Knowing the King

How does understanding Jesus as the *eternal King* change the way you see your daily walk with Him?

Authority Check

Matthew 28:18 says Jesus has all authority. Are there areas of your life where you have not fully submitted to His authority?

Relationship with the King

What does it mean to you personally that Jesus is both your King and your friend?

Cross and Resurrection

How do the cross and resurrection show us the true nature of Jesus' Kingdom compared to earthly kingdoms?

Living it Out

As an ambassador of King Jesus, what is one practical way you can demonstrate His Kingdom in your family, workplace, or community.

Prayer Focus

Thank God for sending Jesus, the eternal King.

Pray for a deeper surrender to Christ's authority in your life.

Ask the Holy Spirit to help you live boldly as an ambassador of King Jesus.

Challenge

Choose one or more areas of your life (e.g., finances, relationships, work habits, or thought life) and intentionally submit it under the authority of King Jesus. Write down one action step you will take to live out His Lordship in that area or those areas.

Kingdom Citizenship

I began this book with **understanding the Kingdom of God**, then I looked at **King Jesus, the Head and ruler of the Kingdom of God**. I am now going a step further into an exciting reality: **Kingdom Citizenship**.

Every kingdom has citizens, and citizenship comes with privileges and responsibilities. It is not automatic; you must meet the requirements of that kingdom. In the same way, we must understand how one qualifies to become a citizen of God's Kingdom, what the process entails, and what is expected of us as Kingdom citizens.

Who Qualifies as a Citizen?

Citizenship in God's Kingdom is not based on nationality, tribe, gender, or social status.

John 3:3 – *"Unless one is born again, he cannot see the Kingdom of God."*

Galatians 3:26-28 - In Christ, all are one; there is no Jew or Gentile, slave or free, male or female.

Revelation 5:9 – Citizens come from every tribe, tongue, people, and nation.

Qualification is not by human merit but by God's grace through Christ.

The Process of Entering the Kingdom

How does one move from being an outsider to becoming a citizen of God's Kingdom?

- *Repentance*

Mark 1:15 – *"Repent, for the Kingdom of God is at hand."*

Repentance means turning away from sin, self-rule, and worldly systems, and turning toward God.

Faith

Ephesians 2:8 – *"For by grace you have been saved through faith…"*

Faith in Christ is the doorway, believing in His finished work on the cross and His resurrection.

- New Birth

John 3:5 – *"Unless one is born of water and the Spirit, he cannot enter the Kingdom of God."*

Citizenship comes through spiritual rebirth, a transformation by the Spirit of God.

This new birth makes us children of God and citizens of His Kingdom (Philippians 3:20).

Entry into the Kingdom is not through religion, rituals, or good works, but through repentance, faith, and new birth in Christ Jesus.

Rights and Responsibilities of Kingdom Citizens

Rights (Privileges)

Access to the King – Hebrews 4:16: We can approach God's throne of grace with boldness.

Heavenly inheritance – Ephesians 1:11: We have obtained an inheritance in Christ.

Divine protection and provision – Matthew 6:33: Seek first the Kingdom, and all these things will be added.

Authority to represent the King – Luke 10:19: We have authority over the enemy.

Eternal life – John 3:16: Citizens are promised everlasting life with the King.

Responsibilities (Duties)

Obedience to the King's commands – John 14:15: *"If you love Me, keep My commandments."*

Living by Kingdom values – Righteousness, peace, love, forgiveness, holiness.

Ambassadorship – 2 Corinthians 5:20: We are Christ's ambassadors, representing Him on earth.

Supporting the Kingdom – Through service, giving, evangelism, and spreading the good news.

Loyalty to the King - our allegiance is first to Christ above all earthly affiliations.

Citizenship is not just about enjoying benefits but also about fulfilling responsibilities.

Application

Do you see yourself as a true citizen of the Kingdom, or are you still living as a foreigner?

Have you truly repented, placed your faith in Jesus, and experienced the new birth?

As citizens, are we exercising our rights (prayer, authority, inheritance) while also fulfilling our responsibilities (obedience, witness, service)?

Summary

Who qualifies as a citizen? All who are born again by grace through faith, regardless of tribe, nationality, or background.

The process of entering the Kingdom – Repentance, faith in Christ, and new birth by the Spirit.

Rights and responsibilities of citizens, we enjoy access to the King, protection, provision, authority, and inheritance, but we are also called to obedience, holiness, ambassadorship, and loyalty to Christ.

Questions for you to Reflect on

Qualification Check

Based on John 3:3, what is the difference between being religious and being a true Kingdom citizen?

Repentance and Faith

How has repentance and faith in Christ changed your identity and direction in life?

New Birth Experience

Can you describe how the new birth by the Spirit has impacted your relationship with God?

Kingdom Privileges

Which right or privilege of Kingdom citizenship do you find most encouraging, and why?

Kingdom Responsibilities

What responsibility as a citizen of God's Kingdom do you feel God is challenging you to grow in right now?

Prayer Focus

Thank God for making you a citizen of His Kingdom through Jesus Christ.

Pray for deeper understanding of your Kingdom rights and courage to exercise them.

Ask the Holy Spirit to strengthen you in fulfilling your responsibilities as a Kingdom ambassador.

Challenge

Intentionally live out your **Kingdom ambassadorship**:

Share your testimony with someone.

Pray for someone in need.

Demonstrate a Kingdom value (forgiveness, love, generosity, peace) in a practical way.

May we not only celebrate our Kingdom citizenship but also live it out daily for the glory of our King.

Kingdom Language & Communication

Kingdom Constitution, Language & Communication

I am now going to move deeper to explore the **Kingdom's Constitution, Language, and Communication.** Every kingdom operates by a set of laws, a shared language, and channels of communication between the king and his people. God's Kingdom is no different.

The Kingdom's Language: Confession, Proclamation, Prayer, and the Word

Confession – Romans 10:9-10 says we enter the Kingdom by confessing Jesus as Lord. Confession acknowledges Kingdom realities and aligns our hearts with the King.

Proclamation – Proverbs 18:21 declares: *"Death and life are in the power of the tongue."* In the Kingdom of God, we proclaim God's promises, blessings, and truth, not fear or defeat.

Prayer – Prayer is the official channel of communication between the King and His citizens. Jesus taught us to pray, *"Your Kingdom come, Your will be done, on earth as it is in heaven"* (Matthew 6:10). Prayer is not begging; it is aligning earth with heaven's agenda.

The Word of God – Hebrews 4:12 reminds us that God's Word is alive and powerful. Speaking the Word in faith activates Kingdom realities in our lives.

The Kingdom has its own language, faith filled words, not idle or destructive talk.

The Power of Words in Shaping Kingdom Reality

In the beginning, God created the world through words: *"And God said…"*

(Genesis 1).

As citizens of His Kingdom, we are called to imitate Him by speaking life.

James 3:5-6 compares the tongue to a small spark that sets a great forest on fire. Words shape destinies, marriages, ministries, and even nations.

When we speak God's Word, we release His authority. Angels respond to the voice of His Word (Psalm 103:20).

Conversely, negative words can cancel Kingdom blessings. That is why Ephesians 4:29 commands us to speak what builds up, not what tears down.

Kingdom citizens must discipline their tongues, using words to align with heaven's will and to manifest Kingdom reality on earth.

The Importance of Scripture as the Kingdom Constitution

Every nation or kingdom has a **constitution**, a supreme law governing its citizens. For the Kingdom of God, that constitution is **the Word of God (the Bible).**

2 Timothy 3:16-17 says: *"All Scripture is God-breathed and useful for teaching, rebuking, correcting, and training in righteousness, so that the servant of God may be thoroughly equipped for every good work."*

The Bible sets out our rights (promises) and our responsibilities (commands). It is both legal document and life manual.

When tempted in the wilderness, Jesus overcame Satan by quoting the constitution: *"It is written…"* (Matthew 4:4-10). If the King Himself used the Word as His authority, how much more should we?

Citizens who ignore the constitution live in ignorance, weakness, and defeat. But those who live by it walk in victory, wisdom, and blessing.

Scripture is not optional, it is the foundation, law, and guide of Kingdom living.

Application

Are your words shaping your life according to Kingdom principles, or are you speaking like the world?

Do you view prayer as Kingdom communication, or just a routine?

Is the Bible truly the constitution of your life, guiding your decisions and priorities?

Summary

The Kingdom's Language – Confession, proclamation, prayer, and the Word of God are the ways Kingdom citizens speak and communicate.

Power of Words – Our words create or destroy; when aligned with God's Word, they shape Kingdom reality in our lives.

The Kingdom Constitution – The Bible is the supreme law of the Kingdom, defining our rights, responsibilities, and guiding us in righteousness.

Reflection Questions

Language of the Kingdom

In your daily life, which do you use more: Kingdom language (faith, prayer, Word) or worldly language (fear, doubt, negativity)?

Power of Words

Can you think of a time when words, either yours or someone else's shaped your reality (positively or negatively)?

Prayer as Communication

How does understanding prayer as aligning earth with heavens will change the way you approach it?

Constitution of the Kingdom

In what ways can you make the Bible more central as the "constitution" of your life?

Living It Out

What one practical change can you make this in your speech, prayer, or Bible engagement to better live as a Kingdom citizen?

Prayer Focus

Ask God to help you discipline your tongue so that your words reflect Kingdom reality.

Pray for a deeper hunger for the Word of God as your constitution and life manual.

Ask the Holy Spirit to help you pray according to God's will, not just personal desires.

Challenge

Practice **Kingdom communication** intentionally:

Replace every negative statement you catch yourself making with a faith-filled confession from Scripture.

Write down one promise from God's Word each day and proclaim it in prayer.

Kingdom Values & Beliefs

Every kingdom has a culture, a way of life that reflects the heart of the king. As citizens of God's Kingdom, we are called to embrace His values and worldview, not the world's. Our beliefs shape our behaviour, and our values reveal where our true allegiance lies.

Core Principles That Guide Kingdom Behaviour

Love – The greatest commandment (Matthew 22:37-39) Jesus replied: "'Love the Lord your God with all your heart and with all your soul and with all your mind. **38** This is the first and greatest commandment. **39** And the second is like it: 'Love your neighbour as yourself.

. Love for God and for people is the foundation of Kingdom living.

Righteousness & Holiness – Matthew 6:33: *"Seek first His Kingdom and His righteousness..."* Our conduct must reflect God's character.

Humility & Servanthood – In God's Kingdom, greatness is measured by service (Mark 10:43-45) Not so with you. Instead, whoever wants to become great among you must be your servant, and whoever wants to be first must be slave of all. For even the Son of Man did not come to be served, but to serve, and to give his life as a ransom for many."

Forgiveness & Mercy – Citizens of the Kingdom forgive as they have been forgiven (Colossians 3:13). Bear with each other and forgive one another if any of you has a grievance against someone. Forgive as the Lord forgave you.

Faith & Obedience – Hebrews 11:6 reminds us that without faith, it is impossible to please God. True faith leads to obedience.

These principles are not optional; they are the DNA of Kingdom citizens.

Kingdom Worldview vs. Worldly Worldview

Worldly worldview: Self-centred, driven by pride, materialism, relativism, and temporary success.

Kingdom worldview: God-centred, rooted in eternity, guided by truth, and concerned with advancing God's purposes.

Romans 12:2 says: *"Do not be conformed to this world but be transformed by the renewing of your mind."*

The Kingdom worldview calls us to see life through the lens of Scripture, not culture or popular opinion.

The way we see the world shapes the way we live in it.

Belief Systems, Ideologies, and Worldviews Shaped by the Gospel

The Gospel does not just save us; it reshapes our entire thinking and living.

Colossians 2:8 warns us not to be taken captive by human traditions and deceptive philosophies.

Instead, the Gospel teaches us Kingdom ideologies:

Life is stewardship, not ownership (Psalm 24:1).

Leadership is service, not domination (Matthew 20:26).

Success is obedience, not accumulation (Joshua 1:8).

Identity is in Christ, not in culture, tribe, or social status (Galatians 2:20).

True Kingdom belief systems flow from the Gospel, not from worldly ideologies.

Spiritual Gifts as Part of Kingdom Identity

Every citizen is given gifts to serve the King's purposes.

1 Corinthians 12:7 – "Now to each one the manifestation of the Spirit is given for the common good."

Spiritual gifts are not for personal glory but for building up the Body of Christ and advancing the Kingdom.

Romans 12:6-8 lists gifts such as prophecy, serving, teaching, encouragement, giving, leadership, and mercy.

Recognizing and using our gifts is part of living out our Kingdom identity and reflecting the values of the King.

Application for Us Today

Do your values reflect the Kingdom or the world?

Are your beliefs shaped more by Scripture or by culture, politics, and trends?

Have you discovered and begun to use your spiritual gifts for Kingdom purposes?

Summary

Core Kingdom values: love, righteousness, humility, forgiveness, faith, and obedience.

Kingdom worldview vs. worldly worldview: God-centred vs. self-centred.

The Gospel reshapes ideologies: stewardship, service, obedience, and identity in Christ.

Spiritual gifts: vital to our Kingdom identity and mission.

Reflection Questions

Values Check

Which Kingdom value do you find most challenging to live out, and why?

Worldview Clash

Where do you see conflict between the Kingdom worldview and the culture you live in?

Gospel & Beliefs

How has the Gospel reshaped one of your personal beliefs or ideologies?

Spiritual Gifts

What spiritual gift(s) do you believe God has given you, and how can you use them to serve the Kingdom?

Practical Step

What is one specific value or belief you will intentionally practice to reflect your Kingdom identity?

Prayer Focus

Pray for a renewal of your mind to see the world through Kingdom eyes.

Ask God to help you embody Kingdom values in daily life.

Pray for the discovery, development, and activation of spiritual gifts within the Body of Christ.

Challenge

Identify one area in your life where you have been influenced by a **worldly worldview,** replace it with a **Kingdom perspective** through Scripture, prayer, and confession.

Practice one **Kingdom value** daily (e.g., forgiveness, generosity, humility) and journal how it changes your interactions.

Kingdom Mindset

I have explored the Kingdom of God, King Jesus, Kingdom citizenship, the Kingdom's constitution, and Kingdom values. I will now explore: **the Kingdom Mindset**.

The mind is the battlefield of the believer. Many Christians struggle with worldly thinking that undermines Kingdom living. Romans 12:2 reminds us: *"Do not be conformed to this world, but be transformed by the renewing of your mind, that you may prove what is that good and acceptable and perfect will of God."*

A Kingdom mindset allows us to think, act, and respond like citizens of the Kingdom, breaking free from cultural and worldly strongholds.

Renewing the Mind (Romans 12:2)

The mind is renewed through **God's Word**, prayer, and the work of the Holy Spirit.

Renewal is not occasional; it is continuous. Daily intake of Scripture and meditating on it transforms our thinking.

Colossians 3:2 – "Set your mind on things above, not on earthly things."

Renewing the mind allows us to discern God's perfect will, rather than being influenced by worldly trends, emotions, or pressures.

Thinking as Kingdom Citizens

A Kingdom citizen thinks differently:

Eternally – Viewing life and decisions through the lens of eternity *(Matthew 6:19-21)*.

Righteously – Letting God's Word guide decisions and actions *(Psalm 119:105)*.

Faith-driven – Believing God's promises rather than circumstances *(2 Corinthians 5:7)*.

Service-oriented – Seeking to bless others and advance the Kingdom *(Mark 10:44-45)*.

Kingdom thinking transforms our priorities, relationships, and responses to challenges.

Breaking Cultural and Worldly Strongholds

Worldly strongholds are mindsets, habits, or belief systems that oppose God's Kingdom. Examples include:

Fear instead of faith

Materialism instead of stewardship

Pride instead of humility

Relativism instead of absolute truth

- *2 Corinthians 10:4-5 – "For the weapons of our warfare are not carnal but mighty in God for pulling down strongholds… casting down arguments and every high thing that exalts itself against the knowledge of God, bringing every thought into captivity to the obedience of Christ."*

Breaking these strongholds requires:

Awareness of the stronghold.

Applying Scripture against the lie.

Consistent prayer and confession.

Renewed thinking aligned with God's Kingdom.

The mind must be disciplined to reflect the values, beliefs, and purposes of the Kingdom.

Application

Identify one area of your thinking that is influenced by worldly patterns.

Begin daily renewing your mind with Scripture, prayer, and positive confession.

Practice Kingdom thinking in decisions, relationships, and priorities.

Break free from cultural or worldly strongholds that hinder your growth in the Kingdom.

Summary

Renewing the mind through God's Word, prayer, and the Holy Spirit.

Thinking as Kingdom citizens – eternally, righteously, faith-driven, and service-oriented.

Breaking cultural and worldly strongholds – identifying, applying Scripture, praying, and capturing thoughts for Christ.

Reflection Questions

Mind Check

Which area of your thinking is most influenced by worldly or cultural patterns?

Renewal Practice

What practical steps will you take daily to renew your mind with Scripture and prayer?

Kingdom Thinking

How can Kingdom thinking affect your decisions at work, home, or community?

Stronghold Awareness

Identify one stronghold in your life. How can you begin to break it using God's Word?

Application Step

What is one tangible action you can take to demonstrate a Kingdom mindset in your daily life?

Prayer Focus

Pray for the daily renewal of your mind.

Ask God to reveal worldly or cultural strongholds in your thinking.

Pray for discernment to align all your thoughts with the Kingdom.

Challenge

Each morning, write down one Scripture to meditate on and confess aloud to renew your mind.

Identify habitual thoughts or perspectives influenced by the world, and counter it with God's truth each time it arises.

Kingdom Roles

I have explored the foundations of the Kingdom, Kingdom citizenship, values, mindset, and the use of spiritual gifts. Now I will focus on **Kingdom Roles**.

Every Kingdom operates according to divine order. Citizens are not independent agents; they function within God's design. Understanding **our roles, gifts, and place in the Body** helps us fulfil our purpose and maintain unity in the Kingdom.

Kingdom Roles and Divine Order

The Kingdom of God has structure and order. While all are equal in value, God assigns roles for governance, service, and mission.

Ephesians 4:11-12 – Christ gave apostles, prophets, evangelists, pastors, and teachers to equip the saints for ministry.

1 Corinthians 12:12-27 – The Body of Christ functions through diversity, with each part playing a crucial role.

The roles God has given in the Kingdom are not about superiority but responsibility, accountability, and cooperation

Understanding Kingdom roles helps prevent disorder and ensures that the Kingdom advances efficiently.

Ministry Gifts and Their Function in the Body

Each believer is endowed with spiritual gifts to serve the Body of Christ and advance the Kingdom.

Romans 12:6-8 – Gifts include prophecy, serving, teaching, encouragement, giving, leadership, and mercy.

1 Peter 4:10 – *"As each has received a gift, use it to serve one another, as good stewards of God's varied grace."*

Functioning in your gift ensures the Kingdom operates as a healthy, unified Body.

Gifts are not for personal glory but for building up others, strengthening communities, and manifesting the Kingdom on earth.

Gender Roles, Kinship Systems, and Group Identity in the Kingdom

God's Kingdom recognizes **distinct roles** while maintaining equality in value and access to God.

Galatians 3:28 – In Christ, there is no distinction in spiritual status; men and women share equal worth and inheritance.

Gender roles in Kingdom service reflect divine design, complementing one another to fulfill God's purposes.

Kinship systems and group identity in the Kingdom:

Believers are part of a spiritual family (Ephesians 2:19).

Church community, mentorship, and fellowship cultivate identity, accountability, and mutual support.

Unity in diversity is a hallmark of the Kingdom; every member has a role, and no role is insignificant.

Application

Recognize and honour God's divine order in ministry, family, and community.

Discover and operate in your spiritual gift to serve others and advance the Kingdom.

Respect complementary roles, whether in gender, mentorship, or group identity, fostering unity and cooperation.

Evaluate whether you are functioning in your God-given role or trying to perform roles outside your design.

Summary

The Kingdom has *roles and divine order* for effective governance and mission.

Ministry gifts are given to serve the Body and advance the Kingdom.

Gender roles, kinship systems, and group identity foster unity, accountability, and cooperation within the Kingdom.

Reflection Questions

Role Awareness

What do you understand to be your God-given role in the Kingdom, in ministry, or in your community?

Spiritual Gifts

How are you currently using your spiritual gifts to serve others? Are there areas of untapped potential?

Hierarchy & Order

How can respecting divine order improve your service and relationships within the Body of Christ?

Gender & Group Identity

In what ways can you honor the roles of others while fulfilling your own Kingdom responsibilities?

Practical Action

What is one step you will take to function more faithfully in your God-assigned role?

Prayer Focus

Thank God for placing you in His Kingdom with a unique role.

Pray for discernment to operate fully in your spiritual gifts.

Ask the Holy Spirit to cultivate unity and respect for roles within your spiritual family.

Challenge

Identify one area where you can serve more effectively in your Kingdom role.

Reach out to a fellow believer to affirm their role or gift in the Body, fostering mutual support and cooperation

Religion & Spirituality in the Kingdom

Religion and spirituality are often misunderstood. In the Kingdom, spirituality is not about empty rituals but about a **living relationship with God**, expressed through sacred stories, Kingdom practices, and moral codes. Understanding these helps us align our lives with God's purposes and participate fully in Kingdom life.

Sacred Stories of Faith in Scripture

The Bible is full of narratives that reveal God's Kingdom and His dealings with humanity.

Stories like Abraham's obedience, Joseph's faith, Moses' leadership, David's trust, and the early Church in Acts illustrate faith, perseverance, and divine guidance.

These sacred stories are not just historical; they also teach **Kingdom principles** and guide our spiritual formation.

Romans 15:4 – *"For whatever was written in former days was written for our instruction, that through endurance and the encouragement of the Scriptures we might have hope."*

Kingdom Practices

Kingdom spirituality is expressed through **practical disciplines** that connect us with God and empower us to live in His Kingdom:

Prayer

Prayer is direct communication with the King. Matthew 6:6 – *"Pray to your Father who is in secret…"*

Prayer aligns our hearts with God's will and activates Kingdom power in the natural.

Fasting

Fasting strengthens spiritual focus and demonstrates dependence on God (Matthew 6:16-18). *"When you fast, do not look somber as the hypocrites do, for they disfigure their faces to show others they are fasting. Truly I tell you, they have received their reward in full. [17] But when you fast, put oil on your head and wash your face, [18] so that it will not be obvious to others that you* are fasting, but only to your Father, who is unseen; and your Father, who sees what is done in secret, will reward you

It is a Kingdom practice that cultivates discipline, humility, and spiritual breakthrough.

Worship

Worship is both adoration and alignment with God's reign. John 4:23-24 – a time is coming and has now come when the true worshipers will worship the Father in the Spirit and in truth, for they are the kind of worshipers the Father seeks. **24** God is spirit, and his worshipers must worship in the Spirit and in truth. Worship in spirit and truth connects us with the heart of the Kingdom.

Sacraments

Baptism and the Lord's Supper are tangible expressions of faith and obedience.

They serve as reminders of our identity in Christ and participation in the Kingdom.

Collective Rituals and Moral Codes

Kingdom spirituality includes **shared practices and ethical standards**:

The early Church prayed together, shared resources, and cared for one another (Acts 2:42-47). They devoted themselves to the apostles' teaching and to fellowship, to the breaking of bread and to prayer. **43** Everyone was filled with awe at the many wonders and signs performed by the apostles. **44** All the believers were together and had everything in common. **45** They sold property and possessions to give to anyone who had need. **46** Every day they continued to meet in the temple courts. They broke bread in their homes and ate together with glad and sincere hearts, **47** praising God and enjoying the favor of all the people. And the Lord added to their number daily those who were being saved.

Moral codes, drawn from God's Word, guide behaviour, protect society, and reflect Kingdom values.

Living ethically and practicing Kingdom rituals together strengthens identity, unity, and witness.

Spirituality in the Kingdom is therefore **both personal and communal**, individual devotion feeds collective purpose, and vice versa.

Application

Reflect on the sacred stories in Scripture and apply their lessons to your life.

Engage actively in Kingdom practices, prayer, fasting, worship, and sacraments, not as ritual, but as relationship-building with God.

Participate in communal spiritual life, respecting moral codes, and supporting the Body of Christ in love and accountability.

Evaluate whether your spirituality aligns with Kingdom principles or merely conforms to empty religious patterns.

Summary

Sacred stories in Scripture guide our faith and formation.

Kingdom practices, prayer, fasting, worship, and sacraments, connect us to God and empower our lives.

Collective rituals and moral codes maintain unity, ethical behaviour, and Kingdom identity in community.

Reflection Questions

Sacred Stories

Which Biblical story has most shaped your understanding of the Kingdom, and why?

Kingdom Practices

How consistent are you in practicing prayer, fasting, worship, or sacraments, and how could you improve?

Collective Rituals

How does participating in communal spiritual life strengthen your faith and accountability?

Moral Codes

Are your daily decisions aligned with Kingdom moral standards or worldly values?

Practical Application

What one Kingdom practice will you focus on this to deepen your spirituality?

Prayer Focus

Thank God for sacred stories and their instruction.

Pray for discipline in Kingdom practices.

Ask God to strengthen your communal participation and moral integrity.

Challenge

Choose one sacred story from Scripture and meditate on it daily, asking God how it applies to your life.

Participate intentionally in one communal spiritual activity (prayer group, worship, or service) to strengthen your Kingdom identity.

Apply one Kingdom moral principle consistently in your decisions and interactions.

Kingdom Social Institutions

I am now going to look at the systems God has designed to reflect His Kingdom on earth.

God's Kingdom is not only personal and spiritual, but it is also social. He establishes families, education, government, economy, and the Church as structures to advance His purposes, cultivate righteousness, and bless communities. Understanding these institutions equips us to live as Kingdom citizens both individually and corporately.

Family as a Kingdom Model

The family is the foundational social unit in God's Kingdom.

Ephesians 5:22-33 – Marriage models Christ and the Church. Husbands love sacrificially, wives respect, and children honour their parents.

Deuteronomy 6:6-7 – Families are primary centres of discipleship, teaching God's Word to the next generation.

Family serves as a **Kingdom microcosm**, shaping character, ethics, and faith.

Kingdom families embody love, service, discipline, and spiritual formation.

Education, Government, and Economy under Kingdom Influence

Education

Education in the Kingdom seeks **wisdom, knowledge, and understanding** according to God's Word *(Proverbs 4:7).*

It trains citizens to discern truth, live righteously, and steward resources wisely.

Government

Romans 13:1-7 – Authorities are ordained by God for justice and order.

Kingdom citizens respect and influence governance, promoting righteousness, justice, and peace.

Leaders are called to serve, protect, and advance God's purposes in society.

Economy

Deuteronomy 8:18 – God gives the power to gain wealth to establish His Kingdom.

Kingdom economics is guided by principles of stewardship, generosity, fairness, and accountability.

Wealth is not an end but a tool to bless others and expand God's purposes.

Role of the Church as God's Kingdom Community

The Church is **the primary social institution of the Kingdom.**

Acts 2:42-47 – The early Church shared resources, prayed, worshiped, and cared for one another.

1 Corinthians 12:12-27 – We get the picture of The Church functioning as a unified body with diverse roles and gifts.

The Church provides fellowship, accountability, ministry opportunities, and societal influence.

It is both a spiritual and social institution, modelling God's Kingdom to the world.

Application

Strengthen your **family as a Kingdom unit** by teaching God's Word, demonstrating love, and practicing service.

Engage with education, governance, and economic opportunities to advance Kingdom principles.

Actively participate in the Church as a Kingdom community, serve, support, and build unity.

Evaluate whether the institutions you participate in reflect God's Kingdom values or worldly patterns.

Summary

Family is the foundational Kingdom model for faith, love, and discipleship.

Education, government, and economy are institutions that can advance Kingdom principles when aligned with God's will.

The Church is God's Kingdom community, providing fellowship, accountability, and societal influence.

Reflection Questions

Family as Kingdom Unit

How can you strengthen your family to reflect Kingdom values and disciple the next generation?

Engaging Institutions

In what ways can you influence education, governance, or economic systems according to Kingdom principles?

Church Participation

How actively are you involved in your Church as a Kingdom community? What role can you play to strengthen unity and service?

Institutional Alignment

Are the institutions you participate in (school, work, church) reflecting God's Kingdom values or worldly patterns?

Practical Action

What one practical step can you take to advance God's Kingdom within a social institution?

Prayer Focus

Pray for families to be strengthened as Kingdom units.

Ask God for wisdom and influence in education, governance, and economic engagement.

Pray for unity, service, and Kingdom effectiveness in the Church.

Challenge

Identify areas in your family, workplace, school, or community where you can actively reflect Kingdom principles.

Engage intentionally in a Church activity or ministry to strengthen your participation in the Kingdom community.

Kingdom Arts & Business

The next aspect I am going to examine is **Kingdom Arts & Business**, areas often overlooked but powerful platforms for advancing God's Kingdom.

The Kingdom is not limited to worship in a church building; it extends to creativity, entrepreneurship, and excellence in every sphere. God equips His people with talents, skills, and creativity to glorify Him, influence society, and expand His purposes.

Music, Literature, and Creative Expression in the Kingdom

Creative expression reflects God, the ultimate Creator (Genesis 1:1-3).

Music: Psalm 150 emphasizes praising God with various instruments. Music uplifts, encourages, and glorifies the King.

Literature & Writing: Proverbs 25:11 – *"A word fitly spoken is like apples of gold in settings of silver."* Words, stories, and publications can teach, inspire, and advance Kingdom truth.

Creativity in the Kingdom is *not just entertainment;* it communicates values, instructs, and inspires action in alignment with God's will.

Business as Ministry

Colossians 3:23 – *"Whatever you do, work heartily, as for the Lord and not for men."*

Business can be an act of worship when conducted with integrity, generosity, and service.

Kingdom businesses:

Provide employment and mentorship.

Fund Kingdom activities and community development.

Reflect God's values of honesty, excellence, and stewardship.

Entrepreneurs are ministers of the Kingdom in marketplaces, demonstrating God's principles through commerce.

Using Talents and Skills for Kingdom Advancement

Matthew 25:14-30 – The Parable of the Talents teaches faithful use of God-given abilities.

Every skill, talent, or profession can serve Kingdom purposes:

Artistic talents inspire and teach.

Professional skills provide service and stewardship.

Technical skills can build tools and systems that advance Kingdom work.

The goal is to *maximize what God has entrusted* to us for His glory and Kingdom expansion.

Application

Identify your creative talents and consider how they can glorify God and influence others.

Approach business and professional work as a platform for Kingdom ministry.

Invest in your skills and talents, not for personal gain alone, but to serve the Kingdom and bless others.

Ask yourself: *Am I using what God has given me to advance His Kingdom, or merely for self-interest?*

Summary

Creative expression, music, literature, and arts communicate Kingdom truth and inspire action.

Business as ministry, Kingdom principles applied in commerce bless others and glorify God.

Talents and skills, every gift from God is to be used faithfully for Kingdom advancement.

Reflection Questions

Creative Expression

How can your artistic or creative talents be used to glorify God and influence others positively?

Business as Ministry

In what ways can your work or business serve as a platform to advance Kingdom purposes?

Stewardship of Talents

What talent or skill have you not fully invested in Kingdom purposes, and how can you begin using it?

Practical Integration

How can you integrate creativity, professionalism, and faith in your daily life to reflect Kingdom values?

Action Step

Identify one tangible step you will take to use a talent, skill, or business platform for Kingdom impact.

Prayer Focus

Thank God for creativity, skills, and professional opportunities.

Pray for guidance on using talents and business to advance the Kingdom.

Ask the Holy Spirit to inspire innovative ways to glorify God through arts and commerce.

Challenge

Choose one creative project or professional skill and dedicate it to Kingdom purposes.

Share your work, skill, or product with someone in a way that reflects Kingdom values and blesses them.

Commit to practicing integrity, excellence, and generosity in every business or professional interaction.

Kingdom Food & Health

The next aspect I am going to focus on is **Kingdom Food & Health**, how God's provision, dietary principles, and feasting shape spiritual, physical, and communal life in the Kingdom.

Food is more than sustenance; it is **symbolic, relational, and spiritual.** The Bible provides principles for diet, communal meals, and spiritual nourishment that guide Kingdom living. Understanding these principles equips us to honor God with our bodies, participate in spiritual fellowship, and reflect Kingdom values through daily choices.

Biblical Dietary Practices and Their Symbolism

Leviticus 11 and Deuteronomy 14 outline clean and unclean foods, teaching discernment and obedience.

Food in Scripture often symbolizes spiritual truths:

Bread = God's provision and sustenance (John 6:35 – "I am the Bread of Life").

Wine = Joy, covenant, and Christ's blood (Matthew 26:27-28).

Paul reminds us that our bodies are temples of the Holy Spirit (1 Corinthians 6:19-20). Eating with wisdom honours God physically and spiritually.

Kingdom dietary awareness is not legalistic; it is about discipline, health, and symbolic alignment with God's will.

The Role of Food in Fellowship, Communion, and Spiritual Discipline

Food is central to fellowship: shared meals cultivate unity, hospitality, and relationship (Acts 2:46).

Communion: bread and wine represent Christ's body and blood, reminding us of His sacrifice (1 Corinthians 11:23-26).

Spiritual discipline: fasting involves abstaining from food to focus on prayer, dependence on God, and spiritual renewal (Matthew 6:16-18).

Meals in the Kingdom are not only physical sustenance, but they also nurture spiritual life, community, and worship.

Lessons from Feasts and Meals in Scripture

Passover (Exodus 12) – Salvation, remembrance, and obedience.

Feast of Tabernacles (Leviticus 23) – God's provision, joy, and gratitude.

Jesus' meals with disciples – Teaching, fellowship, and kingdom revelation (Luke 24:30-31).

Parables of meals (Matthew 22:1-14) – Kingdom invitation, inclusivity, and preparation.

Meals in Scripture teach hospitality, gratitude, unity, and alignment with God's purposes.

Application

Reflect on your dietary choices and their spiritual, physical, and symbolic impact.

Use meals intentionally for fellowship, discipleship, and spiritual growth.

Observe Kingdom feasts and spiritual disciplines (fasting, communion) to strengthen your relationship with God.

Approach food and health as a reflection of stewardship over your body and a Kingdom witness to others.

Key Scriptures

Leviticus 11 – Clean and unclean foods.

John 6:35 – Jesus as the Bread of Life.

Matthew 26:27-28 – Bread and wine in communion.

1 Corinthians 6:19-20 – Our bodies are temples of the Holy Spirit.

Matthew 6:16-18 – Fasting as spiritual discipline.

Acts 2:46 – Fellowship through meals.

Summary

Biblical dietary practices teach discernment, health, and spiritual symbolism.

Food fosters fellowship, communion, and spiritual discipline.

Feasts and meals in Scripture provide lessons on hospitality, gratitude, unity, and Kingdom living.

Reflection Questions

Dietary Awareness

How can your dietary choices honour God physically, spiritually, and symbolically?

Fellowship and Meals

How can you use shared meals to strengthen relationships and discipleship within your community?

Spiritual Discipline

How can fasting or mindful eating deepen your dependence on God and spiritual focus?

Feasts and Lessons

What lesson from Biblical feasts or meals can you apply to your life?

Practical Action

Identify one intentional step you will take to align your food, health, or mealtime practices with Kingdom principles.

Prayer Focus

Thank God for food, provision, and health.

Pray for discipline in diet and spiritual practices.

Ask the Holy Spirit to help meals, fasting, and fellowship reflect Kingdom values.

Challenge

Choose one meal to celebrate God intentionally, giving thanks and reflecting on His provision.

Participate in a communal meal, fellowship, or act of hospitality to strengthen Kingdom community.

If possible, engage in a short fast to focus on prayer and spiritual renewal.

Kingdom Finance

I will now explore **Kingdom Finance**, a critical area where faith, stewardship, and obedience intersect with practical life. Understanding Kingdom financial principles allows us to manage resources wisely, honour God with our wealth, and participate in the expansion of His Kingdom.

Finance in the Kingdom is not just about money, it is about **stewardship, obedience, generosity, and alignment with God's purposes**. The way we handle resources reflects our understanding of God's ownership, provision, and blessings.

Stewardship and Ownership in the Kingdom

God is the ultimate Owner; we are stewards of His resources (Psalm 24:1) The earth is the Lord's, and everything in it, the world, and all who live in it.

Stewardship involves responsible management of time, talent, and treasure.

Luke 16:10-12 – "Whoever can be trusted with very little can also be trusted with much, and whoever is dishonest with very little will also be dishonest with much. **11** So if you have not been trustworthy in handling worldly wealth, who will trust you with true riches? **12** And if you have not been trustworthy with someone else's property, who will give you property of your own?

Faithfulness in small things leads to greater responsibility.

Kingdom citizens recognize that all they have belongs to God and is entrusted to them for Kingdom purposes.

Stewardship requires discipline, integrity, and accountability.

Principles of Giving, Sowing, and Reaping

Giving is central to Kingdom finance and reflects obedience, faith, and trust in God.

Malachi 3:10 – Bring the whole tithe into the storehouse, that there may be food in my house. Test me in this," says the Lord Almighty, "and see if I will not throw open the floodgates of heaven and pour out so much blessing that there will not be room enough to store it. Tithing brings God's blessing and provision.

2 Corinthians 9:6-8 – Remember this: Whoever sows sparingly will also reap sparingly, and whoever sows generously will also reap generously. **7** Each of you should give what you have decided in your heart to give, not reluctantly or under compulsion, for God loves a cheerful giver. **8** And God is able to bless you abundantly, so that in all things at all times, having all that you need, you will abound in every good work. Generous sowing leads to abundant reaping.

Giving is **an investment in the Kingdom**, not merely a charitable act:

It supports ministry, expands the Kingdom, and blesses the giver.

Sowing and reaping also extend beyond finances to time, talents, and influence.

Kingdom Economy vs. Worldly Economy

Worldly economy: Driven by scarcity, competition, self-interest, and accumulation.

Kingdom economy: Driven by generosity, trust in God's provision, abundance mindset, and stewardship.

Luke 6:38 – Give, and it will be given to you. A good measure, pressed down, shaken together and running over, will be poured into your lap. For with the measure you use, it will be measured to you."

Giving produces reciprocal blessing and promotes Kingdom expansion.

Kingdom economy is relational, eternal, and spiritually aligned; worldly economy is transactional and temporal.

Understanding the difference allows believers to *make decisions that reflect God's Kingdom values.*

Application

Recognize God as the Owner of all resources and adopt faithful stewardship.

Practice giving, sowing, and investing in the Kingdom with faith and integrity.

Shift your financial mindset from scarcity and self-interest to Kingdom abundance and generosity.

Evaluate whether your financial decisions honour God and align with His purposes or worldly priorities.

Key Scriptures

Psalm 24:1 – The earth and everything in it belongs to God.

Luke 16:10-12 – Faithfulness in stewardship.

Malachi 3:10 – Tithing and God's provision.

2 Corinthians 9:6-8 – Principles of giving and reaping.

Luke 6:38 – Kingdom economy of reciprocity and abundance.

Summary

Stewardship and ownership – God owns all, and we manage resources as faithful stewards.

Giving, sowing, and reaping – Generosity reflects Kingdom faith and produces blessing.

Kingdom economy vs. worldly economy – Kingdom finances prioritize abundance, trust, and relational investment.

Reflection Questions

Stewardship Awareness

How well are you managing your resources as God's steward?

Giving and Sowing

Are you giving and investing in Kingdom purposes with faith and consistency?

Financial Mindset

Does your financial thinking reflect a Kingdom perspective or worldly scarcity?

Practical Alignment

Identify one area where your financial decisions could better reflect Kingdom values.

Action Step

What one practical step will you take to practice faithful stewardship, generosity, or Kingdom investment?

Prayer Focus

Pray for wisdom and discipline in stewardship.

Ask God to help you embrace generosity and Kingdom-focused financial management.

Pray for opportunities to sow into Kingdom purposes and bless others through your resources.

Challenge

Commit to giving intentionally to a Kingdom ministry or cause.

Review your finances and identify one area where you can practice better stewardship or generosity.

Meditate daily on God's provision and ownership to strengthen your Kingdom financial mindset.

History of the Kingdom of God

I am now going to explore the **History of the Kingdom**, tracing God's work among His people from the nation of Israel to the global Church. Understanding Kingdom history helps us appreciate God's faithfulness, learn from past struggles, and recognize the progression of His Kingdom on earth.

Kingdom history is more than a timeline; it is a narrative of **God's triumph, provision, and guidance**, showing how ordinary people, guided by faith, advanced His purposes.

Shared Narratives of God's People

Israel: God's covenant people, through whom He revealed His laws, promises, and salvation plan (Genesis 12:1-3, Exodus 19:5-6).

The Early Church: Acts 2 – The Holy Spirit empowered believers to spread the Gospel, forming the foundation of the global Church.

Historical examples of people advancing the Kingdom:

David and the establishment of God's kingdom in Jerusalem.

Esther and the deliverance of God's people in exile.

The Reformation and modern missionary movements.

These stories teach **faith, obedience, courage, and perseverance** in advancing God's Kingdom.

Struggles, Victories, and Achievements of the Kingdom

Kingdom work has always faced opposition:

Enslavement in Egypt (Exodus 1-14)

Exile in Babylon (2 Kings 24-25)

Persecution of the early Church (Acts 8:1-4)

Victories include:

The Exodus and conquest of Canaan.

The spread of the Gospel to the Gentiles (Acts 13:47).

Modern global missions and societal transformation through Christianity.

Achievements of the Kingdom are seen in spiritual revival, justice, mercy, and the spread of God's Word.

Challenges are opportunities for growth, faithfulness, and advancement of God's purposes.

The Progression of God's Kingdom on Earth

God's Kingdom has moved from

promise → fulfilment → expansion:

Promise: Abrahamic and Mosaic covenants (Genesis 12, Exodus 19).

Fulfilment: Jesus inaugurates the Kingdom through His life, death, and resurrection (Luke 4:43).

Expansion: The Church spreads the Kingdom to all nations (Matthew 28:18-20).

Kingdom progression involves faithful participation: God works through people to expand His influence on earth.

Today, every believer contributes to the continuation of this history through obedience, evangelism, discipleship, and societal impact.

Application

Learn from the struggles and victories of past Kingdom leaders and communities.

Recognize that we are part of an ongoing Kingdom story, our actions today contribute to God's unfolding purposes.

Be inspired to advance the Kingdom in your sphere, overcoming obstacles with faith, prayer, and perseverance.

Share the stories of God's faithfulness to encourage the next generation of Kingdom citizens.

Key Scriptures

Genesis 12:1-3 – God's covenant with Abraham.

Exodus 19:5-6 – Israel as God's chosen people.

Acts 2 – Birth of the Church and empowerment by the Holy Spirit.

Luke 4:43 – Jesus inaugurates the Kingdom.

Matthew 28:18-20 – The Great Commission.

2 Kings 24-25 – Challenges and exile of Israel.

Summary

Shared narratives: Israel, early Church, and historical examples provide lessons for Kingdom living.

Struggles, victories, and achievements: Kingdom work has faced opposition, but God's faithfulness prevails.

Progression of the Kingdom: From promise → fulfilment → expansion, with every believer contributing to its growth.

Reflection Questions

Learning from History

What lessons from Israel or early Church history can you apply to your life today?

Overcoming Struggles

How can past Kingdom victories inspire you to persevere in your own challenges?

Kingdom Participation

In what ways are you actively contributing to the progression of God's Kingdom?

Faithfulness

How can you ensure that your actions today leave a legacy for future Kingdom generations?

Practical Action

Identify one Kingdom initiative (personal, community, or church-based) that you will commit to.

Prayer Focus

Thank God for His faithfulness throughout Kingdom history.

Pray for courage and wisdom to overcome struggles in advancing the Kingdom.

Ask for discernment to participate effectively in God's ongoing work on earth.

Challenge

Study one historical Kingdom story (Biblical or Church history) and reflect on its relevance to your life.

Share the story with someone to encourage faith and Kingdom-minded living.

Take one practical step to actively contribute to a Kingdom initiative in your sphere of influence.

Eternal Life in the Kingdom

The next aspect I will explore is **Eternal Life in the Kingdom**, the ultimate hope and promise for every believer. Understanding eternal life shapes how we live today, giving purpose, hope, and perspective as citizens of God's Kingdom.

Eternal life is not only a future promise but a present reality through Christ. It invites us to live with **Kingdom priorities, values, and an eternal perspective**, knowing that our labor for God is never in vain.

The Promise of Eternal Life

John 3:16 – Eternal life is a gift for all who believe in Jesus Christ.

Eternal life is relationship with God, beginning now and continuing forever.

1 John 5:11-12 – Eternal life is a present possession through faith in Christ.

It is a life full of peace, joy, and purpose, anchored in God's love and promises.

Believers experience a foretaste of eternal life through spiritual intimacy with God, fellowship, and obedience.

The Fullness of the Kingdom at Christ's Return

Revelation 21:1-4 – God will establish a **new heaven and new earth**, where His Kingdom is fully realized.... And I saw a new heaven and a new earth: for the first heaven and the first earth were passed away; and there was no more sea.

At Christ's return:

Suffering, sin, and death will be defeated.

Justice, peace, and righteousness will reign forever.

God will dwell with His people eternally.

The fullness of the Kingdom reminds us that current struggles are temporary and that **God's eternal purposes will prevail**.

Living with an Eternal Perspective

Colossians 3:1-2 – Set your mind on things above, not on earthly things.

Living with an eternal perspective shapes our priorities, choices, and relationships:

Invest in Kingdom work rather than temporary pleasures.

Value people, relationships, and spiritual growth over material gain.

Practice faith, hope, and perseverance, knowing eternity awaits.

Every decision is weighed against **eternal significance** rather than temporary outcomes.

Application

Embrace the gift of eternal life through faith in Christ, experiencing its power now.

Live in hope and confidence, knowing Christ will return and fully establish His Kingdom.

Let eternity guide daily decisions: invest time, talents, resources, and relationships in ways that reflect Kingdom priorities.

Share the message of eternal life with others, inviting them into God's Kingdom.

Key Scriptures

John 3:16 – Eternal life through belief in Jesus.

1 John 5:11-12 – Eternal life as a present possession.

Revelation 21:1-4 – Fullness of the Kingdom at Christ's return.

Colossians 3:1-2 – Living with an eternal perspective.

Summary

The promise of eternal life – Eternal life begins now through faith and continues forever.

The fullness of the Kingdom – Christ's return will fully establish His eternal Kingdom.

Living with an eternal perspective – Decisions, priorities, and actions should reflect Kingdom significance.

Reflection

Eternal Life

How does knowing that eternal life is a present and future reality affect your daily life?

Kingdom Hope

How can the promise of Christ's return motivate you to live faithfully in the Kingdom today?

Eternal Perspective

Which areas of your life need to be realigned with eternal priorities?

Investing in the Kingdom

How can you invest your time, talents, and resources in ways that have eternal impact?

Practical Action

Identify one decision that you will make with an eternal perspective.

Prayer Focus

Thank God for eternal life through Jesus Christ.

Pray for the Holy Spirit to help you live with an eternal perspective.

Ask God to show practical ways to invest your life for eternal Kingdom impact.

Challenge

Reflect daily on the reality of eternal life and let it shape your decisions.

Identify one Kingdom project, act of service, or relationship investment that has eternal significance.

Share the message of eternal life with at least one person in your sphere of influence.

Let us commit to embracing eternal life, living with hope, and advancing God's Kingdom with eternal significance in mind.

Kingdom Helper

Holy Spirit – Kingdom Helper

John 14:16-17, Acts 1:8, Romans 8:26-27, Galatians 5:22-23

---

a Friend, a Helper, a Comforter; **The Holy Spirit.**

We are living in days of unprecedented change, uncertainty, and challenges. There is confusion, fear, and unrest all around us. And in times like these, the question every believer must ask is: *How do I live as a faithful disciple in a world that seems to be spinning out of control?*

The answer is simple but profound: we cannot do it in our own strength. We need a Helper. We need the Spirit of God. Jesus promised us in John 14:16, *"And I will ask the Father, and he will give you another Helper, to be with you forever."* I want to remind you that the Holy Spirit is not optional. He is essential. He is the Kingdom Helper.

Who is the Holy Spirit?

Many people talk about God the Father and Jesus Christ, but they forget that God also gave us His Spirit His presence in us. The Holy Spirit is not just a force; He is a Person. He thinks, He teaches, He guides, He convicts, and He empowers.

Jesus called Him the Helper, the Advocate, the Comforter. In these days, we need a Helper more than ever. The world will try to guide you with lies, fear, and deception, but the Holy Spirit brings truth. He brings life. He brings power.

Why we need the Holy Spirit in these days

We are living in challenging times. Social media spreads confusion faster than ever before. The economy, politics, even family life, all are under pressure. But the Kingdom of God is not bound by earthly circumstances. The Spirit of God is our secret weapon, our anchor, our guide.

Romans 8:26 tells us that *"the Spirit helps us in our weakness. We do not know what we ought to pray for, but the Spirit himself intercedes for us with groans that words cannot express."*

If you are struggling today, maybe with fear, with anxiety, with a decision you don't know how to make, this is precisely when the Holy Spirit steps in as your Helper. You do not have to figure it all out by yourself. The Helper intercedes, the Helper guides, the Helper strengthens. Be still and let Holy Spirit guide you.

The Kingdom Helper empowers us to live as children of God

Acts 1:8 says, *"But you will receive power when the Holy Spirit comes on you; and you will be my witnesses in Jerusalem, and in all Judea and Samaria, and to the ends of the earth."*

Notice the word: **power.** Not just moral power. Not just knowledge. But supernatural power, the power to overcome sin, the power to love even when it's hard, the power to stand for truth in a culture that mocks righteousness.

In these days, when compromise seems easy, and the world whispers, "It's okay to blend in," the Holy Spirit gives boldness to stand. He gives courage to speak. He gives clarity to act. The Helper equips us to extend God's Kingdom, not just survive in the world.

How to invite the Holy Spirit into our lives

The Holy Spirit is always near, but He waits for our invitation. How do we invite Him?

> Pray for Him daily. Ask, *"Holy Spirit, fill me, guide me, empower me."*

Read and meditate on God's Word. The Spirit uses the Word to teach, convict, and comfort.

Obey Him promptly. When He nudges your heart to forgive, to speak, to help, do it. Obedience is how we grow in intimacy with the Helper.

Yield your life to Him. Do not hold back parts of your heart, your decisions, your dreams. Let the Spirit take full control.

Galatians 5:22-23 reminds us that His fruit; *love, joy, peace, patience, kindness, goodness, faithfulness, gentleness, and self-control*, cannot grow in us apart from Him. In these days, the world desperately needs to see this fruit in God's people.

The urgency of embracing the Helper now

I cannot overemphasize this: the days are urgent. The enemy of our souls is active, working to confuse, discourage, and destroy. But the Kingdom of God is advancing through those who are empowered by the Spirit.

If you rely only on your intellect, your strength, your traditions, you will be overwhelmed. But if you rely on the Helper, you will not only survive, but you will also thrive, and you will be a witness of God's power to a world in chaos.

So, today, I want to call you to a fresh encounter with the Holy Spirit. Do not treat Him as a doctrine or a ritual, treat Him as your Helper, your Guide, your Strength. Pray for a filling of His presence. Let Him empower you to live boldly, to love deeply, and to serve faithfully in these days.

Remember, Jesus did not leave us helpless. He left us the Helper, the Kingdom Helper, who teaches, empowers, and intercedes for us. Receive Him today. Trust Him today. Yield to Him today.

And I promise you, as you walk with the Holy Spirit, you will experience peace in turmoil, clarity in confusion, and **power** to live as a true child of God.

True Kingdom Disciple

Following Christ in Every Sphere of Life

Matthew 16:24-26, Luke 9:23, Colossians 3:17, Romans 12:1-2

What does it mean to be a True *Kingdom Disciple*, a follower of Christ who does not compartmentalize their faith but lives it in every sphere: at work, in the marketplace, in the streets, and in their homes.

Many people say they follow Jesus, but their lives tell a different story. They follow Jesus on Sunday mornings but live by the world's rules the remainder of the time. That is not discipleship. True discipleship is costly. True discipleship requires surrender. And true discipleship demands that we live for Christ *everywhere*, not just in church.

Jesus said in Luke 9:23, *"If anyone wants to follow me, let him deny himself and take up his cross daily and follow me."* There is no "partial discipleship," no "weekend-only" Christianity. In these days, we need a new breed of disciples, disciplined, surrendered, faithful in every place God has called them to.

What is a True Kingdom Disciple?

A true Kingdom disciple is not just someone who prays, sings, and attends church. A true disciple is someone who:

Surrenders their life to Christ daily. This means giving Him control over decisions, plans, and ambitions.

Lives by Kingdom values, not worldly values.

Integrity, honesty, humility, and love are not optional, they are essential.

Acts as a witness everywhere. Matthew 5:16 reminds us, *"Let your light shine before others, that they may see your good deeds and glorify your Father in heaven."*

Discipleship is a lifestyle, not a label. It is a commitment to obey Christ even when it costs us something.

Surrendering in the Marketplace and at Work

The marketplace, the office, the factory, the shop, the online business, is not outside God's Kingdom. Many believers separate "church life" and "work life," but the truth is that God wants you to be His disciple wherever you are.

Colossians 3:17 says, *"And whatever you do, whether in word or deed, do it all in the name of the Lord Jesus, giving thanks to God the Father through him."*

Being a true Kingdom disciple in the marketplace means:

Speaking truth even when dishonesty is profitable.

Treating colleagues with love and respect even when the culture encourages selfishness.

Making decisions that honor God, even if they are unpopular or costly.

Serving customers, clients, and co-workers with excellence as an act of worship.

Your workplace is your mission field. Your boss, your colleagues, your clients, these are the people God has placed in your life for His Kingdom. How you conduct yourself there matters eternally.

Following Christ in Everyday Life

Discipleship does not end at the office gate. It extends to every interaction in life:

At home, we must love and serve our families as Christ loves the Church.

In the streets and communities, we must be peacemakers, helpers, and advocates for righteousness.

In finances, we must honor God in tithes, generosity, and ethical dealings.

In speech, we must be careful not to slander, gossip, or speak harmfully.

Romans 12:1-2 reminds us, *"Offer your bodies as a living sacrifice, holy and pleasing to God, this is your true and proper worship. Do not conform to the pattern of this world but be transformed by the renewing of your mind."*

True discipleship is about surrendering *every part of your life* to Jesus, not just what is convenient, easy, or socially acceptable.

Why it is crucial in these days

We are living in challenging times. The world is more competitive, more corrupt, more distracted, and more dangerous than ever. Temptation surrounds us, the pressure to compromise is high, and the values of the world are constantly infiltrating our hearts.

In these days, Christ needs disciples who will:

Stand firm on truth, even when it costs promotion, popularity, or profit.

Exhibit Kingdom values in a world that often rewards selfishness and greed.

Influence their environments with love, integrity, and wisdom.

Be salt and light in a culture that is losing its way.

The call for Kingdom discipleship is urgent. We cannot afford half-hearted faith. The world is watching, and the Church needs bold examples of surrendered lives that reflect the Kingdom of God.

How to cultivate true discipleship

Being a true Kingdom disciple is a process that requires intentionality. Here is how you cultivate it:

Daily Surrender: Start every day by saying, "Lord, I am Yours. Use me in my home, workplace, and community."

Prayer and Bible Study: Let the Word of God shape your decisions, thoughts, and actions.

Obedience: Don't wait until it's convenient. Obey God in small and big things alike.

Kingdom Focus: Align your work, relationships, and ambitions with eternal purposes.

Community: Surround yourself with other disciples who challenge, encourage, and hold you accountable.

Discipleship is not passive, it is intentional, active, and sometimes costly. But it is the life God calls you to live.

The days demand disciples. Not Sunday disciples. Not "church-only" disciples. But Kingdom disciples, men and women who surrender their lives to Christ in the marketplace, at work, in their homes, and everywhere God has placed them.

Jesus said in Matthew 16:24, *"If anyone wants to follow me, let him deny himself and take up his cross and follow me."* Take up your cross today. Follow Him fully. Surrender every corner of your life. Be a true Kingdom disciple and watch how God transforms not only your life but the world around you.

Fruit of the Spirit

Living through the Holy Spirit as Kingdom Citizens in These Days

Scripture References: Galatians 5:22-23, John 15:4-5, Romans 12:1-2

Something that is central to our Christian walk is: the *Fruit of the Spirit*. Galatians 5:22-23 tells us:

"But the fruit of the Spirit is love, joy, peace, patience, kindness, goodness, faithfulness, gentleness, and self-control. Against such things, there is no law."

Notice, it does not say the *gifts* of the Spirit. It does not say knowledge, prophecy, or miracles. It says *fruit*. This is about character. This is about who we are becoming as we walk with God.

In these days, days filled with stress, division, confusion, and temptation, fruit of the Spirit is not optional. It is essential. If we are to live as true Kingdom citizens, to influence our families, communities, workplaces, and nations for Christ, we must be marked by the fruit of the Spirit.

What is the Fruit of the Spirit?

Fruit is a natural product of a healthy, living tree. In the same way, the fruit of the Spirit is the natural evidence of a life surrendered to Christ. It cannot be manufactured by human effort alone. You cannot create genuine love, joy, or peace by force of will, it must grow from abiding in the Spirit.

Jesus said in John 15:4-5:

"Abide in me, and I in you. As the branch cannot bear fruit by itself unless it abides in the vine, neither can you unless you abide in me. I am the vine; you are the branches. Whoever abides in me and I in him, he it is that bears much fruit."

Notice the key principle: *abiding in Christ produces fruit*. It is a relational process.

It is about intimacy with Jesus, daily surrender, and dependence on the Spirit.

Why the Fruit of the Spirit matters today

We live in days of distraction, division, and pressure. Everywhere we look, there is anger, impatience, and selfishness. Family ties are strained. Workplaces are competitive and cutthroat. Social media amplifies bitterness and pride.

In the midst of this, the world desperately needs Kingdom citizens who carry the fruit of the Spirit. Here is why it matters:

Love: The world is hungry for genuine love, not just words, but action.

Joy: People are searching for hope and contentment that circumstances cannot take away.

Peace: The world is filled with conflict; peace is revolutionary.

Patience and Self-Control: Impatience and impulse are everywhere; self-restraint reflects Christ.

Kindness and Goodness: Integrity and compassion shine when the world is harsh.

Faithfulness: Dependability and loyalty testify to God's faithfulness.

Gentleness: Strength under control, power under humility, this is Kingdom living.

The fruit of the Spirit is not only for personal benefit; it is a testimony to the world. It distinguishes Kingdom citizens from the world.

How to cultivate the Fruit of the Spirit

Many people desire the fruit but do not understand how to cultivate it. Fruit is a process, not an instant gift. Here is how to grow it:

Abide in Christ daily

Prayer, meditation, worship, and reading the Word create intimacy with the Vine.

Without daily connection to Jesus, the fruit cannot grow.

Yield to the Holy Spirit

Galatians 5:16 says, *"Walk by the Spirit, and you will not gratify the desires of the flesh."*

When we obey and submit to His guidance, the Spirit produces His fruit naturally in us.

Practice humility and self-examination

Identify areas where fruit is missing, anger, bitterness, envy, or impatience.

Ask God to transform these areas through His Spirit.

Serve others sacrificially

Love, kindness, and goodness grow through action.

Kingdom fruit is not selfish; it reaches outward, impacting lives around us.

Be consistent and patient

Fruit takes time. Do not give up when you do not see immediate change.

Growth in character is a lifelong process.

Fruit of the Spirit as evidence of Kingdom citizenship

Romans 12:2 reminds us: *"Do not conform to the pattern of this world but be transformed by the renewing of your mind. Then you will be able to test and approve what God's will is, his good, pleasing and perfect will."*

Kingdom citizens are transformed people. We do not mimic the world. We reflect the character of Christ. Our love, joy, peace, patience, and self-control are visible, undeniable evidence that we belong to God's Kingdom.

In these days, being a Kingdom citizen is not just about attending church or knowing Scripture. It is about *how we live, how we treat people,* and *how we influence society.* The fruit of the Spirit is our signature in the world, a mark that says, "I belong to Christ."

Challenges we face today

Living by the fruit of the Spirit in today's world is not easy. The pressures are real:

Temptation to anger and bitterness in online interactions.

Stress and burnout at work, leading to impatience and irritability.

Materialism and selfish ambition threatening our generosity and goodness.

Division and conflict testing our love and peace.

But this is precisely why the Spirit's fruit is crucial. In fact, these challenges are opportunities for Kingdom fruit to shine. When you respond with love instead of anger, patience instead of frustration, and faithfulness instead of compromise. You are living as a true Kingdom citizen in a challenging world.

Conclusion

These days demand more than religious knowledge or rituals. They demand transformed lives, lives marked by the *Fruit of the Spirit*.

If you want to impact your home, your workplace, your community, and your nation for God, it starts with the Spirit working in you. Love, joy, peace, patience, kindness, goodness, faithfulness, gentleness, and self-control, these are not optional; they are essential for living as a citizen of God's Kingdom.

An understanding of the Kingdom of God is essential to establishing our identity in Christ. Add to your knowledge daily.

-Matthew 6:33-

In HIS Love

Peace & Blessings to you!

Autobiography

Valentine Mupfupi is a passionate Kingdom teacher and visionary leader dedicated to equipping believers, building Kingdom-centred communities, and advancing the gospel across nations. As the founder of Kingdom Churches International, he carries a clear mandate to raise disciples who understand their identity, purpose, and authority in Christ. His life mission is to see God's Kingdom transform families, cities, and nations through intentional Kingdom influence.

Valentine is the author of two books: Wash Your Brain, which explores the concept of Brain Hygiene, and The Fast Life, which unpacks the principles of prayer and fasting. And this latest book, **Kingdom Gospel**, empowers readers to embrace the principles, power, and life-changing relevance of the Kingdom of God in their daily walk.

In addition to ministry, Valentine is also a Kingdom entrepreneur with over 20 years of experience in Sales and Marketing across various industries, contributing significantly to business development and organizational growth.

www.ingramcontent.com/pod-product-compliance
Lightning Source LLC
Chambersburg PA
CBHW061437300426
44114CB00014B/1726